Practical
Business Continuity
Management

Top Tips for
Effective, Real-World
Business Continuity Management

Andy Osborne

Practical
Business Continuity
Management

Top Tips

for

Effective, Real-World

Business Continuity Management

Andy Osborne

First published 2007

© Andy Osborne

Published by Word4Word, Evesham, UK

www.w4wdp.com

The right of Andy Osborne to be identified as the
author of this work has been asserted by him in
accordance with the Copyright, Design & Patents Act
1988.

ISBN-978-1-906316-01-3

A CIP catalogue record of this book is available from
the British Library.

Printed in the UK by Cromwell Press.

Contents

About the Author

An acknowledged expert in the field of business continuity management, Andy Osborne has spent almost twenty years helping many and varied organisations, across a broad range of industry sectors, to develop, implement, prove and maintain their business continuity capability. Andy regularly presents on business continuity and risk management in the UK and Europe.

Andy is an active member of the Business Continuity Institute (BCI) and is the founder and chairman of the BCI's UK North Midlands Forum, one of the most popular and well attended of the regional forums.

In 1997, Andy formed the consultancy practice Acumen, which is now established as one of the most well-known and respected business continuity consultancy firms in the UK.

Andy lives in Evesham with his wife, two children, one dog, assorted chickens and ducks, and several thousand bees! He confesses to being a keen gardener and beekeeper and an enthusiastic, though largely untalented golfer, guitarist and juggler.

To contact Andy or to book him for consultancy work or speaking engagements, e-mail him at aosborne@acumen-bcp.co.uk.

Foreword

By Lyndon Bird, Technical Services Director, Business Continuity Institute

As Technical Services Director of the Business Continuity Institute I am regularly asked to review new books or papers on the various facets of business continuity management (BCM). Many of these publications are interesting, well written and meet an ever increasing need for more information about this vital subject. What most of them lack, however, is an immediate impact for the casual business reader - what the marketing experts might call "the elevator pitch".

In reading Andy Osborne's work I immediately felt that at last we had the book we needed to engage with the moderately interested business professional, rather than simply adding more words for the specialist BCM practitioner to argue about. I have often opined that in many ways BCM could be called "Basic Commonsense Management" because what we say and do is not really controversial. When the ideas behind BCM are properly explained to a newcomer to the subject, their reaction is often surprise that organisations do not do it already, with questioning about why they do not.

There are many suggested reasons why organisations do not always give BCM the attention it needs, but most of the reasons centre around a number of misconceptions such as "it is only for large companies", "it is only another piece of compliance red-tape", "our management are used to handling crises on the fly", "it is an insurance issue" or "it has never happened to anyone in our industry/sector/location", etc.

Once you have read this book I think you will re-assess your views on all of these assumptions and will understand why BCM is necessary and how it fits seamlessly into the management armoury of important skills. Yet this book is about tips not techniques, about insight not facts, about vision not methodologies. In fact above all it is about an experienced practitioner happy to share what he has learned without enhancing his writing with unnecessary jargon and academic pretension. If you want a textbook to tell you how to do a business impact analysis, undertake a cost benefit analysis on various recovery options or manage a complex BCM development project this is not for you. However, if you want to know what business continuity is really about I suggest you read this book several times, and perhaps even give a copy to your boss as a present. If he or she reads it, it might well make your life much easier.

Introduction

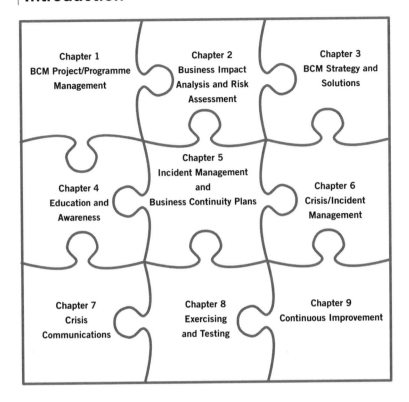

This book is aimed at anyone with responsibility for, or involvement in, developing, maintaining or testing their organisation's business continuity management (BCM) programme. Most of all, it's aimed at people who want to get past the theory – people who have to undertake their BCM activities in the real world.

Whether you're a project manager tasked with implementing the BCM programme, a senior manager responsible for your department's continuity plan, an IT or facilities manager looking after the infrastructure elements, or a business continuity manager co ordinating the various activities, this book is for you!

This book won't tell you how to "do" BCM. It won't give you chapter and verse on the various elements of the BCM process. It won't bang on about "lifecycles" or "methodologies" or "benchmarking" or "best practice" – there are plenty of books around that do that, if that's what you want. What it will do is give you dozens of helpful, practical tips to use at various stages of your BCM programme – tips that will help you, as they have helped others, to make your BCM programme a success.

Recognising that readers may well be at different stages of their own BCM programme, and have different needs or issues to resolve, the tips in this book are grouped so as to enable the reader to easily find those that are most relevant to their own situation at any given time. The chapters, each of which relates to one piece of the BCM "jigsaw", are shown in the diagram on the previous page.

However, this is not really a book that's meant to be read from start to finish. Rather, the reader is encouraged to dip in and out as the need or fancy takes them.

Chapter 1
BCM Project/Programme
Management

Tips in this chapter:

"Friends in high places"
"Project or process?"
"Project yourself"
"Top down, bottom up"
"How do you eat an elephant?"
"A cunning plan"
"Horses for courses"
"You can't have one without the other"

"Planning is an unnatural process; it is much more fun to do something. And the nicest thing about not planning is that failure comes as a complete surprise, rather than being preceded by a period of worry and depression."

Sir John Harvey-Jones

Friends in high places...

If you haven't done so already, go and find yourself a senior management sponsor, preferably someone on the board. And make sure everyone knows a) who this is and b) how much importance they place on business continuity management.

Executive commitment is an absolute must. Without it you'll be swimming against the tide. However, you'll be surprised how much interest people will take in your project if the chief executive or managing director shows an interest too.

Project or process?...

Well, both really. While it is essential to manage the business continuity management implementation project as you would manage any other significant project, there are elements of business continuity management which must ultimately become ongoing processes and become ingrained in people's day to day activities. Examples include backups and offsite tape movements, plan reviews and updates, exercising and testing, to name but a few – these should all be seen to be part of people's normal jobs and not an afterthought. And if you can get these activities into their job specifications and objectives, so that they form part of the appraisal and bonus system, people will have a vested interest in making sure they actually do them!

Project yourself...

Who'd be a business continuity manager?

You spend ages doing business impact and risk analyses, developing and implementing a strategy, and conducting awareness and training campaigns. Then the first new project comes along and no-one even considers business continuity requirements until the project has been signed off and is underway! Sound familiar?

To avoid this you need to make business continuity management part of the project management lifecycle for all projects. In particular, due consideration needs to be given to risk, continuity and recovery issues at project initiation.

Whether you're moving to a new office, implementing a new IT system or changing a business process, the business continuity implications need to be considered up front, not as an afterthought.

It's much easier (and often cheaper in the long run) to build the continuity solution in at the design stage than to try and retro-fit it later.

So why not start making your life easier and talk to your project management people today?

Top down, bottom up...

There are two things that are almost guaranteed to scupper the business continuity planning process from the outset. The first is a lack of senior management commitment. The second is a lack of commitment from the business users.

Many well-meaning business continuity managers try to overcome the absence of either (or both) by producing the business continuity plans by themselves. A common result is ineffective plans that sit on a shelf gathering dust, which aren't updated to reflect changes within the business and which are seldom, if ever, tested.

To be successful, business continuity management requires a top down, bottom up approach. There needs to be visible commitment at board level, which should set and communicate policy. Implementation of the policy and the associated strategies and plans needs to be the responsibility of the business, not just the business continuity manager.

Easier said than done, perhaps, but if you can achieve these two things, you'll have a fighting chance of success. Without them, life can be very difficult. So, if you haven't done so already, why not start your quest for an executive sponsor today?

How do you eat an elephant?...

Despite the best efforts of some dodgy characters to convince you otherwise, business continuity management isn't actually rocket science. But despite the fact that the BCM process is relatively straightforward, it can seem a bit daunting to the newcomer as there can be quite a lot of it.

But ask yourself this question - "how do you eat an elephant?". The answer is "one piece at a time". The trick is to carve up the elephant into manageable slices.

There are several distinct slices within the BCM lifecycle, including analysis and strategy, plan implementation, awareness and so forth. And each of these can be sliced up further, into activities such as business impact analysis, risk assessment, crisis management team selection, IT or business recovery planning and training, to name but a few. And several of these could be further sub-divided by location, or business unit if appropriate, to the organisation in question.

In fact, there are any number of ways that the BCM elephant can be sliced up, allowing discrete and manageable chunks to be assigned to various "diners". The trick is to give priority, particularly in the early stages, to those that give the best return for the effort put in. And that means just a little bit of menu planning, *before* launching into the first course.

A cunning plan…

Business continuity management is about writing a business continuity plan, right?

Wrong! It's about putting in place a continuity *capability* that meets the needs of the business, of which the plan is a small (albeit important) part. This involves far more than simply writing a plan.

It's about:

- Understanding the requirements of the business, which means some form of business impact analysis and risk assessment;
- Implementing an appropriate strategy and solutions to meet those business requirements;
- Putting in place a sound incident management capability;
- Educating staff so that everyone (particularly key players) knows their roles and responsibilities;
- Documenting the plan (in a form that's actually usable if it has to be activated for real);
- Exercising and testing to ensure everything actually works;
- Managing change and keeping plans and the underlying strategy and solutions up to date.

So while the plan is important, it's the planning process that really matters.

As Dwight D. Eisenhower is quoted as saying, "Plans are nothing; planning is everything." Which sums it up nicely really.

Horses for courses...

If you have the luxury of appointing a business continuity manager, careful consideration should be given to where the role should sit. Often, the IT department is seen as a good place, one reason being that they may already have some IT recovery plans or solutions in place.

However, it's usually better for the business continuity manager's role to reside within the business, rather than the IT department. Otherwise, there's a danger that business continuity is seen as an IT issue rather than a business issue and, consequently, of the business failing to get properly involved.

All too often, inappropriate solutions are implemented by well meaning IT departments working from an invalid set of assumptions. No disrespect to IT people, but the business generally knows best what the business needs, so engaging them fully in the process is essential.

So think carefully about where the business continuity function should sit within the organisation. Either way, it's crucial that IT and the business work in partnership if the business continuity programme is to be successful.

You can't have one without the other...

Why is it that in organisations with the luxury of having both a business continuity manager and a risk manager, the two more often than not see their roles as being completely separate? And, as a result, they don't talk to each other very much.

There's often a debate about whether risk management is part of business continuity management or vice-versa. But whichever camp you're in, the bottom line is that you just can't have an effective business continuity capability without managing your risks. And you can't have effective risk management without a business continuity strategy and plan.

Business continuity management and risk management are two sides of the same coin. Business continuity management is essentially a combination of risk management and contingency planning. And risk management involves contingency planning as a key mitigation method for certain types of risk.

However you look at it, business continuity management and risk management are inextricably linked and, like love and marriage, you can't have one without the other – at least not if you want your business continuity management and risk management to be anything like effective.

Follow-up actions

This page is for you to note which tips in the previous section struck a chord and the follow-up actions you intend to take to benefit your own business continuity management programme in your own organisation.

Tip/page...	To make this tip work for me I will...

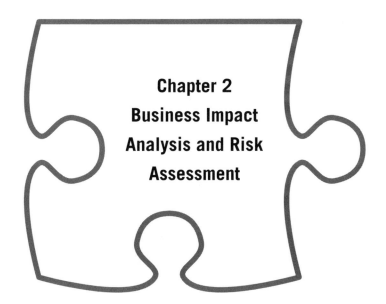

Chapter 2
Business Impact
Analysis and Risk
Assessment

Tips in this chapter:

"Time is money"

"A risky business"

"The name of the game"

"Analysis paralysis"

"Prevention *and* cure"

"The outer limits"

"Joining forces"

"A source of embarrassment"

"Just mind your own business?"

"The most elegant forms of managerial decision involve problems that never have to be solved because they are prevented from occurring...they are anticipated and side-stepped.

The deliberate non-catastrophe is one of the most effective contributions a manager can make."

James Martin

Time is money...

A truism if ever there was one. In particular, downtime costs. And the costs are not necessarily purely financial. The cost to your reputation could be equally damaging - in some cases even more so.

But how much does downtime actually cost, and how much should we therefore be investing in risk mitigation measures and contingency arrangements?

A business impact analysis will provide the answers to the question "How much do we stand to lose?". In addition it will identify critical resources and recovery/continuity requirements over time. As a result, you'll be in a position to make *informed* decisions on how much you should invest in solutions, and develop an appropriate business continuity strategy for your business, rather than taking a "finger in the air" approach.

A risky business...

Risk is unavoidable. All businesses, whatever their size, are constantly faced with risks, large and small. Indeed, businesses can only prosper by successful risk taking. The objective for any business must therefore be to strike the correct balance between risk and potential reward. The aim is to manage risk appropriately, not to eliminate it.

The best way to do this is to make risk management part of the business culture. Everyone within the organisation has a part to play. By using a few simple techniques, all departments can identify the risks to their part of the operation and put in place countermeasures to reduce the impact of the most serious.

Risk assessment is not just the domain of the professional risk manager or business continuity manager. It is an important management tool that can be used at all levels within the organisation.

In the battle against risk, doesn't it make sense to have a whole army on your side?

The name of the game...

When conducting a business impact analysis (BIA) there are two important words to keep in mind: *business* and *impact*. It may sound obvious but, strangely, this is often forgotten and the BIA gets confused with a risk assessment.

The BIA is the part of the business continuity process that determines the level of pain an organisation would suffer if it were unable to carry out its critical processes. We're not really interested in all the possible reasons why at this stage - that's what the risk assessment is for. And anyway, if the BIA's done properly, there's enough to think about without trying to do a risk assessment at the same time.

So don't make your life more difficult than it needs to be. Concentrate on business impacts during the BIA, then conduct a separate risk assessment to identify potential risks to the critical processes identified by the BIA. Remember, it's called a business *impact* analysis - the clue's in the name!

Analysis paralysis...

It's widely accepted that the business impact analysis and risk assessment are critical initial activities in the business continuity management programme. Indeed, they provide the basis on which the business continuity strategies and plans are built.

But it is possible to get too hung up on the analysis, with the result that subsequent activities are seriously delayed. It has been known for this phase to take so long that by the time it's complete the business has changed and the results are no longer valid. It's usually because those doing the analysis try to be too precise or too scientific. They get bogged down in detail and lose sight of the fact that the analysis is the means to an end, not the end itself.

In a rapidly changing environment it can be difficult to hit a moving target. But where business continuity management is concerned, it's often better to be roughly right than precisely wrong.

So keep it simple, keep it short and sweet, and aim to get things roughly right.

Prevention *and* cure...

A large part of business continuity management is concerned with developing recovery strategies and plans that would come into play in the event of a disaster or major incident. Indeed, for many business continuity managers, this is their raison d'être.

However, a point that is often overlooked is that prevention is usually better than cure. Clearly not all disasters can be prevented, and there is still a need for recovery strategies and plans. But by managing our risks we can lessen the probability of a disaster occurring in the first place, or reduce the impact of an incident to "non-disaster" proportions.

Business continuity management is about risk management and contingency planning, not just one or the other. A sound business continuity programme will address both of these key issues. And an effective risk management programme will go a long way towards making your business more resilient and lessening the possibility of having to invoke your recovery plans.

So why have a disaster if you don't have to?

The outer limits…

Many business continuity plans aim to cater for the "worst case scenario". But what exactly is meant by "worst case"? For many it's the loss or unavailability of a single building or facility, while for others it could include significant loss of staff or be a city-wide disaster. And who knows, some of the pessimists among us might even be planning for the end of the world as we know it!

Before launching into the development of business continuity strategies and plans, it's worth taking a while to think about exactly what you're planning for, in the form of the "maximum survivable incident" for your organisation. There's probably little point in spending huge amounts of time and money planning for anything bigger if there's no way you could recover from it anyway.

Sometimes, we have to accept that there are some things that are just too big to plan for. Setting and agreeing the boundaries early on will help you to focus your attention and could save you some wasted effort in the long run.

Joining forces...

As with business continuity management in general, risk management is much more effective if a top down, bottom up approach is adopted.

It's all very well for executive management to make statements in the annual report about how wonderful the risk management system is, but that in itself doesn't make the organisation more resilient. If it isn't backed up by action then it's not worth the paper it's written on.

A successful risk management approach requires a two-pronged attack, which includes buy-in from both the executive and business managers. Yes, there needs to be commitment at board level, but the business also needs to be involved to make it happen.

The most successful organisations in this respect are the ones who manage to embed risk management in their culture – where executive support is visible; where risks and associated mitigation measures are identified at all levels; where risk registers are maintained by departmental managers and team leaders; and where risk management is seen by all employees as just a normal part of the way they do their jobs.

So what's it to be – splendid isolation or a joined-up approach that actually makes a difference? The choice is yours.

A source of embarrassment...

Many organisations choose to outsource certain activities, for various reasons. They may consider them to be non-core activities, want to outsource a particularly specialist or risky process, or do it purely to save money.

Outsourcing can make good commercial sense, but only if the implications and risks are properly understood.

Several organisations have suffered serious embarrassment or damage to their reputation owing to an outsourced supplier's failure to deliver. Whether it's IT, manufacturing, call centre, purchasing, delivery of products or whatever, someone else's problem can quickly become yours.

If things go wrong your customers will turn to you, not your supplier. You might have outsourced the process, but you retain the risk, and the responsibility, and the reputation, and the hassle if things go wrong.

So make sure your decision to outsource is an informed one. One that includes a thorough risk and impact assessment, and an understanding of the supplier's own continuity plans.

Just mind your own business?...

Many business continuity strategies are very inward looking and insular, concentrating only on the risks to, or impacts associated with the loss of the organisation's own processes, locations, staff, etc. However, if you are reliant on other businesses (such as key suppliers or customers) you need to consider the potential impact on your business if they should suffer a problem. For instance:

• If a particular supplier is unable to deliver critical components, can you source them from elsewhere, and do you have sufficient stocks to tide you over?

• If a major customer stops ordering for an extended period, what impact will this have on your business?

If an impact analysis shows that you would be significantly affected you need to do something to mitigate the risk, including:

• Making contingency arrangements, such as finding alternative suppliers or holding extra stock;

• Checking whether the other party has its own business continuity plans and risk management systems in place;

• Checking whether your insurance would provide some level of recompense.

So think of others as well as yourselves, and don't let someone else's problem become your problem.

Follow-up actions

This page is for you to note which tips in the previous section struck a chord and the follow-up actions you intend to take to benefit your own business continuity management programme in your own organisation.

Tip/page...	To make this tip work for me I will...

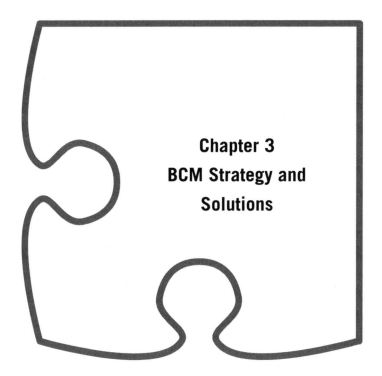

Chapter 3
BCM Strategy and Solutions

Tips in this chapter:

"Location, location, location"
"Don't let it get your backup"
"Do your homework"
"Mirror, mirror"
"Out of harm's way"
"Safe as houses?"
"It ain't necessarily so"
"Double trouble"
"Virtually everything you need"

"However beautiful the strategy, you should occasionally look at the results."
Winston Churchill

Location, location, location...

When selecting a recovery site, careful consideration should be given to its location. In particular, the distance from the live site is important. Too close and you risk it being affected by the same incident that denies access to your site. Too far away and staff may be unwilling to travel there in the event of an "invocation".

There are no hard and fast rules, and much will depend on your own location, type of business and specific risks, but factors to consider include:

• Accessiblity: does it have good access by road, rail or air? Is access more difficult at certain times of the day or days of the week?

• Services: are power, water, gas, telecommunications, etc provided from a different source (sub-station, exchange, etc.) to the primary site?

• Risks: is it subject to the same risks as the primary site. For instance, is it in the same flood plain or earthquake zone?

Whether you use a third party recovery site or one of your own, you need to ensure it will be available to you if you need it, and that your staff can actually get to it, within a sensible time.

Ask any estate agent - they'll tell you that location is everything!

Don't let it get your backup...

Your computer backups and vital records are, by definition, critical to your recovery in the event of a disaster. So it is absolutely essential that they are accessible if they are ever needed in an emergency.

Some common practices, which could compromise the availability of these items, and therefore your ability to recover, include:

• Storing them onsite. Although a fire safe offers some protection, many incidents result in a denial of access for several days or even weeks. If you can't get to them you can't use them!

• Storing them offsite but too close to home. Offsite storage should at the very least be outside any potential emergency services cordon (which could be 500 metres or more), but preferably further.

• Not removing backups from site in a timely manner. Typical causes include leaving the previous day's tape in the drive until the next backup is started, backups remaining onsite for many hours until it is convenient for someone to transport them, or the people who move them not understanding the importance of their role.

• Bringing backup tapes back onsite for day-to-day file recoveries. Disaster backups should mean just that – if backups are required for day-to-day operational problems then a second, onsite backup should be taken or a process developed to allow restores to be done without physically returning tapes to site.

To ensure availability of your backups and vital records they must be:

• Stored offsite;

• Taken offsite as soon as possible;

• Remain offsite until the retention period has expired.

When push comes to shove, if you don't have your backups and vital records, how will you recover your business?

Do your homework...

Home working is often seen as the panacea for business recovery. "All our staff can work from home" is a phrase often heard during the business impact analysis.

But can they really? There's a huge difference between sitting at your kitchen table for a few hours once every couple of months to write a report and actually working from home all day, every day, for any length of time. And if people don't actually work from home now, how can you expect to implement what amounts to a significant change to their working environment and business processes at the time of a crisis and expect it to work seamlessly?

On top of the practical considerations, there are also likely to be health and safety, insurance and management implications, among others. Then there's the small issue of facilities – the office and IT equipment, network links, paperwork, etc. required to do the job. Let alone the impact on the family. All these things need to be thought about.

So a little bit of homework is required, in the form of a feasibility study, to determine whether home working really is a viable solution. And proper planning is needed to implement a proper solution. Oh, and it needs to be tested to confirm that it actually works.

All this means there are likely to be some costs involved. But if you get it right, there may also be significant business benefits aside from those related to business continuity.

Mirror, mirror...

Offsite mirroring of data on critical IT systems is great! No more loading and unloading of tapes. No more remembering to send tapes offsite and bring them back at the right time. And, depending on the method of mirroring employed, the data on the backup system can be bang up to date and/or restored almost instantaneously.

But there's a small point that is sometimes overlooked. If you ever need to invoke the backup system in the event of a problem with the primary, how do you then back it up? Unless you have a second mirror of your data, or can set one up extremely quickly post-invocation, the data on your now live system is at risk.

So don't consign the humble tape backup to the scrap heap. While you might not want to do tape backups as well as mirroring, at least consider maintaining the ability to do them, so they can be switched back on if needed. And by the way, don't forget to test them periodically to make sure they still work.

Out of harm's way...

"We have a clear desk policy but no one adheres to it" is a common lament heard during business impact analysis interviews or risk assessment workshops. As is "We don't have enough cupboards to put things away" or "We don't have a big enough fire safe to hold all our critical documents, so what's the point?".

Well the point is that this kind of apathy results in many organisations putting their critical information at risk.

People often think that if they don't have a fire safe there is nothing they can do to protect their critical documents. But simply putting documents away at the end of the working day, or when they're not being used, actually offers a fair degree of protection and can dramatically increase their chances of survival in the event of a fire, flood, explosion or whatever.

Documents filed in an ordinary wooden or metal cupboard or filing cabinet, or in a desk drawer, are much better protected than those left out on desks. Think about it – they don't catch fire as easily, they take much longer to burn, they don't get as wet, they don't blow around and they're safer from prying eyes than loose documents on desks.

So if it's important to you, put it away – or one day you may find you've become a paperless office without intending to!

Safe as houses?...

Many organisations store their computer backups and other vital records onsite in a fire safe.

While fire safes offer some protection and can serve a useful purpose, they do have their limitations and these need to be understood when weighing up your options. Points to consider include:

- Different types of safes offer different levels of protection, in terms of the duration and the temperatures they will withstand. A severe or prolonged fire may well exceed these tolerances.

- Computer media and paper are not the same and need different levels of protection. A fire safe designed to protect paper will almost certainly not offer adequate protection for computer media.

- Not all fire safes are waterproof, so when the fire brigade come and douse the burning building with thousands of gallons of water the contents of the safe can be ruined anyway.

- The fire safe is often stored in the basement, which can make it difficult to get to after a major incident such as a fire (see also the above note about water, which tends to flow downwards!).

- In a denial of access situation, you may not be able to get to your backups and vital records at all for a significant period.

- Many fire safes are not resistant to severe impact, such as that caused by an explosion, or the safe falling through the floor during a fire.

- Fire safes are not the same as security safes. Additional security may be required to ensure sufficient protection from theft.

In most cases, the best option is to store backups and vital records offsite, at least as far away as the extent of any potential police cordon (sometimes 500 metres or more). But if this option really isn't open to you, don't be lulled into a false sense of security and at least be aware of the risks you may be exposed to.

It ain't necessarily so...

When putting together our business continuity strategies and plans we often have to make a number of assumptions. One of the most common is that key people will:

- Be available;
- Be willing and able to up sticks at a moment's notice;
- Be happy to work long hours, miles from home for several weeks.

Unfortunately, experience has shown that when it comes to the crunch this isn't necessarily the case. So, when developing your business continuity strategy and associated plans, try to guard against disappointment and risk to the recovery by:

- Involving people early in the planning process, making them aware of the potential issues and taking notice of the feedback;
- Carefully considering the location(s) of your proposed recovery site(s);
- Not making the recovery plans reliant on particular individuals;
- Considering alternative sources for provision of staff (e.g. via agencies or other parts of the organisation);
- Cross-training.

Your people are probably the most important element in your plan and, more to the point, your organisation's survival. Make sure you don't overlook the potential issues. And don't put your business at risk by making assumptions without validating them.

Double trouble...

Splitting your IT equipment across multiple computer rooms is a good way of increasing resilience and reducing your risk, right? Not necessarily!

Unless system components are duplicated or mirrored to give true resilience, you might actually be lulling yourself into a false sense of security.

Many systems have a number of inter-related components, and loss of any one of them would stop the system working. If this is the case, simply splitting them across different rooms may actually increase the risk of failure, as there are now two or more environments that can go wrong.

Rather than spending your money on a second computer room, it may be a wiser investment to spend it on increasing the environmental protection and controls at your existing location instead. At the very least, ensure you do a proper risk assessment before making the decision.

So this is a case where it might make more sense to keep all your eggs in one basket, but to make the basket itself safer.

Virtually everything you need...

During the implementation of their business continuity strategies and plans, many organisations will put together a "battle box", containing all the vital information and other stuff that they're likely to need to enable effective incident management and recovery. This is a splendid idea.

For some organisations, however, ensuring access to the "battle box", particularly out of hours, can present some challenges, as can keeping the information in it up to date. Even selecting a location that's far enough away not to be affected by the incident but near enough to get to in a hurry isn't always easy.

So why not consider supplementing the physical battle box with a virtual, online version?

A couple of secure web pages, hosted offsite, can do the job admirably, perhaps with some general information that's available to all staff (with the correct password, of course) on one page, plus some department or team-specific pages (each with its own password) for information that you want to restrict access to.

There will always be a place for the physical battle box. After all, it's difficult to store pieces of equipment online! But supplementing it with a virtual battle box can help ensure that your vital information is available when you need it most.

Follow-up actions

This page is for you to note which tips in the previous section struck a chord and the follow-up actions you intend to take to benefit your own business continuity management programme in your own organisation.

Tip/page...	To make this tip work for me I will...

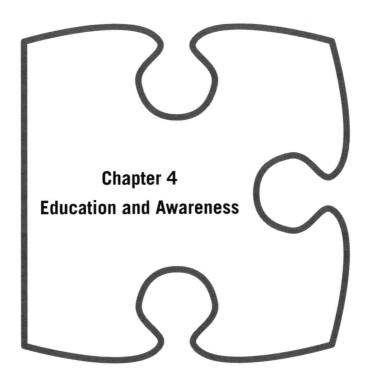

Chapter 4
Education and Awareness

Tips in this chapter:

"The missing link"
"Education, education, education"
"Blissful ignorance?"
"Familiarity breeds content"
"By all means"
"As clear as mud"
"Carpe diem"
"It's not big and it's not clever!"
"Ready, willing - but able?"
"Once is not enough"
"Sack the business continuity manager!"

"Chance favours the prepared mind."

Louis Pasteur

The missing link...

It's amazing how many people see business continuity management as something that's on the fringes of normal business activity. It's something that's done by the business continuity manager or the IT department, not them, and it certainly isn't part of their day-to-day business life.

Although most people understand what the word "business" means in the context of their own organisation, and most understand the meaning of the word "continuity", for some reason putting the two words together conjures up a vision of some sort of black art that they don't understand or have any interest in.

But the clue's in the name - *business* continuity, i.e. the continuity of their (and your) business. And until the link is made between business continuity management and what they do as part of their normal job, the danger is that this attitude will persist and the business continuity efforts will be unsuccessful.

Easier said than done maybe, but for business continuity management to be really effective it needs to become ingrained as an element of normal business processes. Indeed, it needs to be part of the culture of your organisation. Which means it needs to start at the top.

Education, education, education...

Many organisations get hung up on the goal of producing "the plan" as the be-all and end-all of their business continuity project.

But the plan itself won't save the business in the event of a disaster. What will save the business is the right people making the right decisions and performing the right actions at the right times. The purpose, albeit vital, of the incident management and recovery plans is to provide supporting information to this process.

If the right people don't know who they are, or what they need to do, or what is actually in their plan, or what issues they may come up against when they invoke it, recovery will at best be severely hampered and at worst may not happen at all.

"The plan" should therefore be seen as merely the documented presentation of management competence. The importance of training and awareness, and exercising of the plans and the people involved, cannot be over-emphasised.

It therefore follows that a significant amount of effort needs to go into the education process – an important point that is, sadly, often overlooked.

Blissful ignorance?...

Ignorance may be bliss but, when it comes to recovering from disaster, ignorance can be fatal.

If your staff, particularly the key players needed for incident management or recovery, are unaware of your strategies and plans and their roles and responsibilities within them; if they don't know who to contact, where to go or what to do when they get there, your chances of survival may be slim.

Having a plan is not enough. People need to know about it, know what is expected of them and have practised its operation.

So if you haven't done so already, embark on your training and awareness campaign today. Use every means at your disposal, from roadshows to mouse mats, from workshops to mock disasters, to get your message across. You need to raise awareness at every level within the organisation, from the chief executive to the receptionist.

Ignorance may be bliss, but knowledge is power. More power to your survival!

Familiarity breeds content...

It's a fair bet that you've invested significant time and effort in the production of your business continuity plans. But these documents will be worthless in the event of a disaster if the people called upon to use them don't know what's in them or what's expected of them.

It's not the plans themselves that will keep your business going in the event of a problem, it's the people who will use them. It therefore goes without saying that the more familiar they are with the plans and the more practised they are at activating them, the greater the chances of success when it comes to the crunch.

Awareness, training and exercising are vital elements of a successful business continuity management programme. Neglect them at your peril!

By all means...

Each year, one week in March[1] is designated by the Business Continuity Institute as "Business Continuity Awareness Week", so why not use this as an opportunity to raise awareness within your own organisation?

A comprehensive awareness and education programme should ensure that everyone within the organisation, from the chief executive to the administration staff, knows about the existence of your business continuity plans and their roles and responsibilities within them. Methods you could try include any, or indeed all, of the following:

• Roadshows and seminars;

• Executive and staff briefings;

• Newsletters, guidebooks and leaflets;

• Exhibition stands or displays in prominent places;

• Videos;

• Training courses and workshops;

• Incident management and business recovery exercises;

• Business continuity-related quizzes or competitions;

• Screen savers;

• Mouse mats;

• Intranet sites...

...in fact, anything and everything that gets the message across.

So whatever you decide is appropriate for your organisation, use every means at your disposal to spread the word. The more people who are in the know, the more chance you have of ensuring success.

And one last thing. Whatever you choose to do for Business Continuity Awareness Week, don't forget that there are another fifty one weeks in each year will you?

---

[1] Applies to the UK and Europe. A different month is often chosen in the US, Australia and the Middle East, and this may vary from year to year.

As clear as mud...

When developing your business continuity plans (and even more so when actually using those plans to respond to a crisis) it's essential that everyone involved understands them and their associated roles and responsibilities. Misunderstandings can scupper even the best laid plans, and should be avoided at all costs.

It's therefore important that:

- The incident management and business continuity plan structure is simple and straightforward;
- The plans themselves are concise and easy to use (even in the midst of a crisis);
- Roles and responsibilities are clear and unambiguous and the people concerned actually know what's expected of them;
- Continuity and recovery capabilities and service levels (i.e. what will be provided and when) are clearly understood by the business, with no scope for misunderstanding.

However, merely writing these things down and asking people to read them when they have a spare minute is not enough.

A programme of awareness and education that informs people and keeps them up to date, along with regular exercises and rehearsals to bring the key players up to speed and keep them there, are essential components of your business continuity management programme.

If you think clarity isn't important, here's a quote from Richard Nixon that might make you think again...

"I know that you understand what you think I said, but I am not sure you realise that what you heard is not what I meant."

Now if that doesn't make it clear, nothing will!

Carpe diem...

The first few hours following a disaster or major incident are crucial. Actions taken (or not taken) then can make or break the recovery. Get this right and the chances are you'll be in control. Get it wrong and you could well find yourself on the back foot, reacting to circumstances rather than controlling them.

It is essential that valuable time isn't lost in the early stages of your response and recovery. Achieving this requires everyone involved to know their roles and responsibilities. It means knowing who to contact, where to go, what to do and how and when to do it. And it means being able to lay your hands on the vital records required to support your actions, when you need them.

This means pre-planning and preparation. It means recovery plans that are easy to use and up to date. Just as importantly, it means training and awareness, and familiarity with those plans. And it means an ongoing programme of exercising and testing to ensure recovery strategies actually work and key players are up to speed.

We all hope we never have to invoke our recovery plans for real. But if you do, make sure you're ready and able to seize the initiative.

It's not big and it's not clever!...

BCM, BCP, RTO, RPO, BIA, CMT, IMT, MCA, MTPD,[1] etc., etc....
what on earth is that all about?

In common with many industries, the business continuity world
is awash with acronyms, abbreviations and jargon. And while this
is all very well for your average business continuity manager or
consultant when they're speaking to another business continuity
"expert", actually most business users aren't fluent in BCM-speak.

Put yourself in their shoes for a moment. If someone came to you
asking you to do a whole load of seemingly new or additional stuff,
who at best seemed to want to blind you with science and at worst
appeared to be speaking complete and utter gobbledegook, how
would you feel?

So if you want to engage the business, rather than having them
glaze over when you talk to them, then why not speak in terms
that the business understands? Otherwise there's a risk that the
business won't buy in to what you're trying to do, or there will be
misunderstandings that can scupper your plans.

---

[1]Just in case you were wondering: BCM = business continuity management; BCP = business continuity plan; RTO = recovery time objective; RPO = recovery point objective; BIA = business impact analysis; CMT = crisis management team; IMT = incident management team; MCA = mission critical activity; MTPD = maximum tolerable period of disruption (aaaargh!)

Ready, willing - but able?...

Someone once said that "the world is run by people who turn up". The trouble is that sometimes the people who turn up aren't necessarily the ones you'd choose to run the world!

In incident management and business recovery terms, you don't just want a random bunch of misfits and prima donnas to turn up. You want the right people, with the right skills and abilities, who can actually do the job for you.

Therefore, it's not good enough just to come up with a few names and write them in a plan. People need to know what's expected of them. They need to be aware of the issues that they might be asked to deal with. They may need training to enable them to do this. And they certainly need to exercise or rehearse.

So, if you ever need to invoke your business continuity plans, you need to be confident that the right people will not only turn up, but that they will also know what to do when they get there.

Once is not enough...

Like Christmas and (unless you're the Queen) your birthday, Business Continuity Awareness Week comes around but once a year. We might look forward to it with eager anticipation. We may even plan things well in advance to maximise our enjoyment of the event. We may even ignore it and hope that it goes away!

And, as with Christmas and birthdays, it is possible to over-indulge so that people get a bit sick of it and are actually glad when it's over.

But why wait a whole year, binge for a short period and then forget all about it until next year?

When it comes to your business continuity management awareness campaign the best approach might well be to do it little and often. Why not do something every month (or even every week) to keep people thinking about business continuity management throughout the year?

Sack the business continuity manager!...

An ex-director of British Airways was once quoted as saying
"Business survival is everybody's job, just as customer service
is everyone's job. If you have a business continuity manager you
should sack them."

A teeny bit extreme maybe, particularly given that in most
organisations there wouldn't be any business continuity
management without the business continuity manager.

But there's a serious point here. And the point is that in many
organisations, business continuity management isn't seen as being
part of everyone's normal job. So they seldom think about it, let
alone practise it. Because that's the job of the business continuity
manager, isn't it?

Our friend at British Airways went on to say "...if you have a
customer service manager you should sack them now!" But most
organisations, even though customer service might be ingrained
in the culture, still need a customer service manager to drive the
process forward, to ensure a consistent approach and to help with
awareness and training and all those other good things that actually
make it work.

So the business continuity manager *is* an important person, and
perhaps sacking them wouldn't be a great move. But we do need
to ensure that everyone in the business – and that's *everyone,* from
the CEO down to the office junior – understands that business
continuity management is an important part of their normal day
job. It's not the role of (and actually, it's not possible for) the
business continuity manager to do it for them.

Follow-up actions

This page is for you to note which tips in the previous section struck a chord and the follow-up actions you intend to take to benefit your own business continuity management programme in your own organisation.

Tip/page...	To make this tip work for me I will...

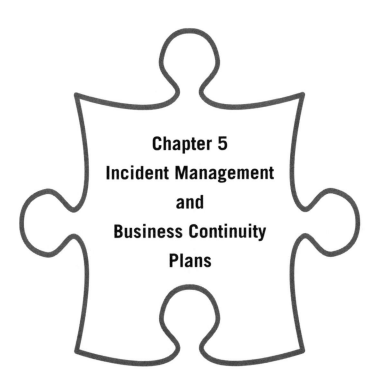

Chapter 5
Incident Management
and
Business Continuity
Plans

Tips in this chapter:

"Easy peasy?"
"One size fits all"
"The best laid plans"
"One up, one down"
"External influences"
"Less is more"
"Don't fall into the trap"
"A break in continuity"
"Knowing me, knowing you"
"Appreciating assets"
"A little can go a long way"

"The only thing harder than planning for an emergency is explaining why you didn't."

Unknown

Easy peasy?...

Writing a business continuity plan is a piece of cake these days isn't it? A quick trawl of the internet will turn up several plan templates that you can download, or you could try and get hold of another organisation's plan from one of your friends or acquaintances. Then all you need to do is insert your organisation's name and contact details and Bob's your uncle, there's your plan.

Clearly this is utter nonsense! However, it's surprising, if not a mite worrying, that some people actually adopt this approach. But it's missing the point somewhat. And the point is that there's a huge difference between a business continuity *capability* and a business continuity *plan*. Developing that capability means *planning* as opposed to just writing a plan. It means having a strategy and implementing solutions. And, among other things, it means involvement from the business, using education and awareness and exercising and testing, to develop, instil and prove that capability.

Filling in your details in someone else's document might make you feel like you've got a plan. Just don't expect it to actually work when you need it will you?

One size fits all...

One decision that has to be made when developing your business continuity plan is whether to have separate plans for different scenarios or to try and produce one plan that caters for all possible situations.

The problem with the first approach is that it is almost impossible to predict the disaster scenario that will result in your plans being invoked. Experience has shown that more often than not, the disaster that was planned for isn't the one that has to be recovered from. Producing numerous plans in an attempt to cater for every possibility can result in an administrative nightmare.

Unless there are specific threats to your particular business which warrant their own specific plans (e.g. train/plane crash, product recall or specific technology failure) then it probably makes sense to take a more generic approach and make your plans flexible enough to cater for any situation.

Napoleon said, "No plan ever survives contact with the enemy". Being too prescriptive in your planning can be prohibitive to the recovery. What will get you through is having a plan that is flexible enough to cater for any given situation and a team with the ability, authority and training to deal with whatever the incident throws at them.

The best laid plans...

People, place and plans are the three vital elements for recovery in the event of a disaster or major incident. So you've written your plans and made provision for your recovery site, whatever form that may take. But what if key staff are not available? Do your plans depend on specific individuals?

Don't assume that people will automatically be available or willing to rush to your assistance in the event of a problem - experience has shown that this is not necessarily the case, for a variety of reasons. Better to remove those dependencies now, for instance by cross training, better documentation or enlisting the help of third parties, than find yourself wanting when the chips are down.

One up, one down...

When developing business continuity plans it can be helpful to put yourself in the shoes of the people with whom you'll need to interact if the plans are ever used "in anger" (or in an emergency).

If plans are invoked, each level in the incident management hierarchy will need to communicate with others, both above and below their own level. For instance:

- The incident management team will need to communicate upwards with the executive team and downwards with the business recovery teams.

- The executive team may have to deal with shareholders, the parent company or the government, as well as providing strategic direction to the incident management team.

- Business recovery team leaders need to understand the pressures that the incident management team may be under as well as considering the needs of their own staff.

So don't develop your plans in a vacuum. Whichever recovery team you may find yourself in, when developing your own plan, think very carefully about the actions required to achieve not only your own team's objectives, but also those of the next level up. Consider also what assistance you can give to the level below yours, to ensure the actions they take will impact positively on your own objectives.

Thinking one level up and planning one level down will ensure plans are developed in the context of "the bigger picture", resulting in incident management and recovery being more effective.

External influences...

When putting together your business continuity plans it's not uncommon to concentrate on the elements directly within your control and ignore the outside world. But external influences can scupper even the best thought out plans.

The emergency services and other public authorities will take control following a large-scale incident or disaster. Their priorities of saving lives, minimising damage and apprehending criminals may not necessarily fit with your own business recovery priorities.

It is therefore a good idea to talk to these external agencies, including the police, fire officer and the council's emergency planning officer, before the event, during the plan development phase. Being aware of how the emergency services and other public bodies will act should ensure that your own procedures are more effective.

So don't wait until they're too busy dealing with a disaster to talk to you!

Less is more...

When documenting the business continuity plan, there can sometimes be a desire, particularly for the inexperienced business continuity manager, to produce a huge weighty tome in the mistaken belief that it'll look impressive, thereby justifying the effort that's gone into it.

The trouble is, not many people are going to read through a plan that's two feet thick, and those that do are unlikely to remember much of it. So the first time that many people see it in all its glory will be when they're trying to use it in anger. And it won't work!

The business continuity plan shouldn't be an exercise in verbosity. A good plan isn't measured by its bulk or its weight. A good plan is one that's actually usable when it's needed. Something that's concise and simple to follow; that contains the important information but no superfluous padding; that the relevant teams are familiar with and comfortable with.

This may, in fact, take a bit more effort than the big fat plan, not least in the education that needs to go with it. But it should result in an effective strategy, rather than a huge white elephant.

Don't fall into the trap...

"The backlog trap" is a phrase often used to describe the effect on a business of the backlog of work that builds up when a system or process is unavailable, and the length of time it takes to reduce that backlog. It's possible to express the backlog trap by way of a clever formula, but a good rule of thumb is that it can take four or five times the length of the outage to process the backlog and get back to normal.

It therefore stands to reason that the longer the downtime, the longer the recovery. Or to put it another way, the sooner you're in control, the less time it'll take to catch up. Sounds simple, but many recovery plans overlook or underestimate the effort and resources required to process the backlog.

So make sure your incident management plans are effective, so that valuable time isn't lost in the early stages of your response and recovery. Ensure your recovery strategy enables you to get back up and running in time to avoid the backlog trap. And ensure your recovery plans consider just how you will catch up with the backlog and who will do this.

A break in continuity...

During holiday periods, one of the main assumptions of many BC plans – that key staff will be available and contactable – may not actually hold true.

A small amount of pre-planning could help avoid a situation where the ability to respond effectively is compromised.

Actions to consider include:

- Finding out when key staff will be on holiday, whether they are going away and whether (and, if so, how) they can be contacted;

- Appointing additional deputies to key people/roles (or even deputies to deputies) to ensure sufficient cover is maintained;

- Ensuring that anyone drafted in to cover temporarily is fully aware of their roles and responsibilities and is given any necessary training;

- Checking that contact details are up to date (both for permanent and temporary team members) and that any temporary changes to normal contacts are identified and recorded;

- Ensuring that any interim arrangements are communicated, particularly to "first responders" such as security or facilities staff.

Disasters and crises don't take holidays. A bit of forethought could make the difference between success and failure if the plan has to be invoked while your key people are taking their well earned break.

Knowing me, knowing you...

A previous tip[1] discussed the "post disaster" priorities of the emergency services and other public authorities.

These organisations can be a great source of information during your recovery planning stage. For instance:

- The council's emergency planning officer can provide you with information on how their response to a major incident will be co-ordinated;

- The police can advise on the extent of any cordons which may be put up;

- The crime prevention officer can provide you with statistics on crime within your area to aid your risk management process.

Establishing relationships now could pay dividends later. For example:

- Getting to know the fire officer and providing floor plans showing any hazardous areas could potentially gain you access to your building sooner;

- Allowing the fire brigade to use your premises for training exercises will not only help build a relationship but also means they will be more familiar with the layout of the site;

- Establishing contacts with the various bodies (police, fire brigade, emergency planner, city authority, etc.) could improve access to crucial information in an emergency.

It can be helpful to make these people aware of your organisation's recovery plans, maybe even lodging a copy with them.

So, establish those relationships now. After all, it's not just what you know that counts - it's who you know too!

---

[1] External influences (see page 64)

Appreciating assets...

"Our people are our greatest assets" is a popular phrase. And it's true that many organisations do indeed highly value their people. But it's also true that, sometimes, the degree of consideration shown to staff during recovery from a disaster or major incident is not as high as during "business as usual".

In the heat of battle it can be easy to forget that people are only human. While many will perform above and beyond the call of duty when called upon, people generally don't like being taken for granted.

Experience has shown that despite a successful recovery, in a number of cases, the organisation concerned has subsequently lost many good people because they didn't feel valued. This is particularly true of staff deemed "non-critical" and therefore not directly involved in the early stages of recovery. The main complaints were that they felt unimportant or ignored and didn't really know what was going on.

So avoid using terms like "critical" and "non-critical" in your continuity plans. Think carefully, before the event, about how best to deploy people post-disaster. Don't assume that people will be happy to sit at home and twiddle their thumbs indefinitely. Ensure people know what's expected of them and why. And, if you do ever need to invoke your recovery plans, make sure that people are, as far as possible, kept involved and kept informed.

Your people may well be your greatest asset, particularly when it comes to business continuity. So look after them if you want them to look after you.

A little can go a long way...

All your key players have their own copy of the business continuity plan, right? And they all keep a copy offsite like you asked them to, don't they? And they all religiously keep it in their briefcase/home/car/at the golf club/with them in the pub (delete as applicable) don't they? Of course they do...except when they don't!

The problem is that most business continuity plans are fairly sizeable documents (some more so than others, but that's another story[1]), at best running to several pages. And with the best will in the world it's often just not practical for people to keep it with them all the time, wherever they go.

But a business continuity plan needn't necessarily be a large, detailed document. It may be possible to reduce the key information needed in the early stages of its activation to a single sheet of paper. Something that can be folded into three and kept in a pocket perhaps – you know the sort of thing? Or maybe even that's too big for some. So how about a fold-out, concertina-style document that ends up half that size, or less? Or even a credit card-sized piece of card or plastic containing some simple instructions and basic contact details.

The possibilities are almost endless. All it requires is a bit of imagination – and, as importantly, a bit of thought about what information is absolutely essential.

---

[1]Less is more (see page 65)

Follow-up actions

This page is for you to note which tips in the previous section struck a chord and the follow-up actions you intend to take to benefit your own business continuity management programme in your own organisation.

Tip/page...	To make this tip work for me I will...

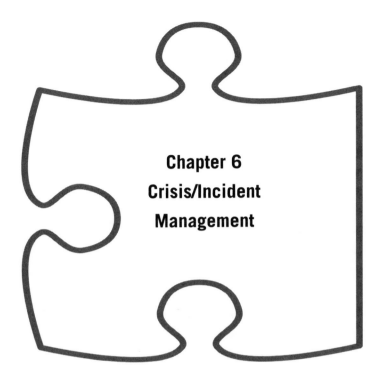

Chapter 6
Crisis/Incident
Management

Tips in this chapter:

"When written in Chinese the word crisis is composed of two characters. One represents danger and the other represents opportunity."

John F Kennedy

Crisis? What crisis?...

The importance of effective crisis management cannot be overstated. But if we're going to effectively manage a crisis, we really ought to know when we're having one!

The characteristics of a crisis include :

• An urgent need for decisions;

• A lack of accurate information on which to base those decisions;

• An acute shortage of time;

• Insufficient resources at our disposal;

• Uncertainty of the outcome.

You could argue that for some organisations this is business as usual! But we're not talking about day-to-day management headaches here. Crisis management is about dealing with extreme situations. Stuff that's outside the scope of normal business problems. Stuff that might well threaten life and limb or the future of the business. Stuff that's outside the scope of "normal" management experience.

Managing a crisis is not the same as normal day-to-day business management. It needs specific skills and abilities. It needs sufficiently trained and experienced people if it's to be effective.

So make sure your crisis management team are up to the job and prepared for it should a real crisis ever strike.

War and peace...

"Organise for peace, but prepare for war" is an army adage that is as applicable to business continuity planning in the business world as it is in the armed forces. It reflects the fact that exceptional circumstances call for a different way of doing things to the norm.

During peacetime the army has a certain organisation and mode of operation. However, at the drop of a hat (or a bomb!), they change their organisation and individual roles to ones more suited to the new situation. This is not an easy thing to do, and it requires everyone concerned to be fully trained and practised in the wartime mode. It requires a commanding officer with the necessary skills and experience to effectively manage operations. And it requires a huge amount of training, so during peacetime they run regular exercises.

In the commercial world, crisis or emergency management is not the same as "business as usual". It too requires a different organisation (crisis management structure) and a different way of doing things (crisis management plans). It requires a strong crisis manager, with the necessary skills and authority, and supporting team members who are fully trained and have rehearsed their plans until they are almost second nature.

So why not take a tip from an organisation that is well versed in crisis management? And while we all hope that peace will prevail, if war does break out you'll be prepared.

The right stuff...

One of the key decisions to be made when putting your business continuity plans together is who should lead the incident or crisis management team. It can also be one of the trickiest.

Often, the most senior person in the incident management team is given the role by default. But while the person needs to be senior enough to have some "clout", seniority in itself isn't enough. The qualities that make a good operational manager don't necessarily guarantee a good crisis manager.

Good crisis managers are able to take quick and decisive action, often under extreme pressure. They are natural leaders, who command respect and are able to motivate a team. They need to be flexible and adaptable as well as being highly motivated themselves. And they need to be excellent communicators, at all levels.

A background in command and control may be an advantage, and there may be other more suitable candidates within the organisation than the most senior manager. Consider, for instance, ex-military or ex-police officers who may have some of the required attributes, although a good knowledge of the business is also needed. And beware, this can be a sensitive subject, often involving internal politics, which may have to be handled tactfully.

In a crisis, having the right person in charge could be the difference between success or failure. So think carefully, and choose your crisis manager wisely.

The information gap...

One of the characteristics of a crisis is the need to make urgent decisions against a background of acute time pressure and insufficient accurate information.

Much of this information relates to the specific circumstances of the incident, over which we may initially have little control. But there is some information that we do have control over and making sure that this information is available to the crisis management team in a timely manner can reduce the amount of decisions that have to be made "on the fly".

As Donald Rumsfeld so eloquently put it "...there are known knowns; there are things we know we know. We also know there are known unknowns; ...we know there are some things we do not know..."

The type of information we can control (the "known knowns") includes where to go and who to contact. It includes contact details, maps and inventories. And it includes actions to take in certain circumstances along with agreed triggers for key actions.

Prior planning, tightening procedures, proving them by rehearsal and keeping critical information up to date and available can all go a long way to easing the crisis decision making process.

So sort out the "known knowns" now and give the crisis management team a fighting chance with the unknowns.

A commanding position...

"Command Centre", "Control Centre", "War Room" – call it what you will, in the event of a disaster or major incident this will be a very important place. It will be the location from which the recovery operations are directed and managed. It will be staffed by senior people, probably working long hours and under stressful conditions. So it makes sense to plan its location and facilities in advance.

When setting up your command centre, consider the following:

- Availability – it may need to be available at very short notice, in the middle of the night or at the weekend;

- Location – it should be reasonably near to, but far enough away from, the disaster or incident site, to still be easily accessible;

- Access – keyholders should be available and contactable;

- Facilities – including desks, chairs, telephones, fax, PCs, network connections, meeting rooms, whiteboards, radio, TV and video, stationery and catering supplies. And, if possible, it should have separate meeting, quiet work and rest areas;

- Alternatives – consider nominating more than one location, in case the primary location is unavailable for some reason.

And having decided on suitable locations, do be sure to let all the relevant people know where they are and how to get there!

Ready for inaction?...

Why would anyone go to all the trouble of setting up their incident management team, assigning roles and responsibilities, briefing the team members, writing and rehearsing plans and then, when an incident occurs which has the potential to escalate into a crisis, ignore the fact that the incident management team exists?

Well, for some reason, this is precisely what a lot of organisations do! In many cases the incident management team either don't convene at all, or only get together when the situation has become so bad that they are constantly on the back foot, reacting to rather than proactively managing the incident.

The problem is often the fact that sound escalation procedures don't exist or, worse, that the incident management team see themselves as something akin to the cavalry, charging in to save the day when the situation is almost hopeless!

But wouldn't it be better if they came together earlier, to assess the situation calmly and plan the response rationally? And if the incident doesn't then escalate to epic proportions, then so what? They can always stand down. But if it does, there's more chance that they'll be ready for it and the chances of recovery are likely to be higher.

So if they're there, why not use them. If nothing else, it's good practice for them...and practice makes perfect doesn't it?

Questions, questions...

When a crisis hits, and particularly in the early stages, there are usually more questions than answers. The crisis management team can feel like they're working in the dark, having to make difficult decisions with insufficient information on which to base them (described as "the information gap" in a previous tip).

But there are two small questions that the team can ask, which can help enormously in managing the crisis - "what if?" and "so what?" In other words, what might be the consequences of a particular decision or if a particular event occurs? And are the consequences acceptable?

Asking these two simple questions at various stages throughout the incident response and recovery process helps the crisis management team to be proactive rather than purely reactive. It allows potential problems to be anticipated and risks to be identified and assessed, enabling solutions or containment actions to be planned *before* the event. Crucially, it can allow the team to start planning effectively right from the word go, even when at first sight there seems to be very little information to go on.

One other question to end with - why not give it a try during your next crisis management exercise?

Don't panic...

The decision to invoke your business continuity plans in the event of a huge, disastrous incident such as a major fire, flood, explosion, earthquake or hurricane is a "no-brainer". It's pretty obvious that all is not well when your building has flames coming out of every window, or is a smouldering hole in the ground, or is under ten feet of water.

But many "disasters" aren't sudden and dramatic. They creep up on the unsuspecting victim. What starts as something seemingly innocuous escalates, often through a combination of events, into something far more serious than first suspected. And these creeping disasters can catch an unprepared incident management team on the hop, so that by the time they've convened and invoked their plans the situation has got away from them. And once this has happened it can be extremely difficult to regain the initiative and regain control.

But if the incident management team is smart and convenes earlier on in the process, before the situation has reached epic proportions, it is far more likely to get, and remain, on top of the situation. It's therefore far better for an incident management team to "over-react" and stand down if they're not required than under-react and be left high and dry.

So, although there's no need to panic at the slightest minor problem, an effective escalation process and an incident management team that's on the ball will ensure a readiness to react promptly and kick the recovery into action before it's too late.

Read all about it...

Despite the existence of a carefully crafted incident management and recovery plan, many an incident management team has been known to forget all about it at the time of a crisis (real or exercise) and "ad lib" their way through events with little or no reference to the document.

While the plan document itself is not the be-all-and-end-all of the business continuity planning process, and it shouldn't necessarily be slavishly followed, it is nonetheless an important document that supports the incident management decision making process and helps to ensure that nothing gets forgotten.

To ensure that the plan is not completely overlooked in the heat of the moment, while still allowing the incident management team room to be flexible, responsive and creative, one approach is to assign a member of the team to take a step back from proceedings and to track through the plan as events unfold. In this way they can prompt the team when they feel that following a particular part of the plan would be helpful, or when the plan contains information that would be useful in resolving a particular issue. They can also help keep things on track and make sure nothing important is missed.

So think about who in your incident management team should carry out this activity, brief them and update the roles and responsibilities in the plan accordingly. Oh, and you might even like to try it out during your next incident management exercise.

A mountain of paperwork...

Ever seen the state of an incident management control centre in action? They can get very messy! Typically, a huge amount of paper is generated and left lying around, partly because it may be needed later, partly because everyone has a copy of almost everything, and partly because everyone's too busy to dispose of it. Add this to the equipment scattered about – PCs, printers (generating more paper), fax machines (still more paper), not to mention coffee cups and pizza boxes – and you have a recipe for clutter and inefficiency.

So what can be done about it? Well, there are a few things that can help.

- Get it on the walls: use flipcharts, wallcharts, whiteboards, etc. to get the stuff that needs to be visible to everyone off the table and up where it can be seen.

- Get it on the system: if information needs to be logged for future reference, get it in electronic format as soon as possible rather than lying around on bits of paper - but don't forget those backups!

- Get rid of it: appoint someone to file the stuff that needs to be kept and to cull that which is surplus to requirements - but remember, some of it may contain confidential information that needs to be disposed of appropriately.

- Share it: do you really need fifteen full copies of the entire recovery plan? Or are one or two full copies sufficient, with key extracts held by those who need them?

- Keep on top of it: be disciplined and regularly review what's needed and what's not.

It may seem trivial now, but anything you can do to make the control centre run more efficiently will pay dividends at the time of a crisis.

The main thing...

When managing the response to an incident, or performing business or IT recovery activities, it can be very easy for those involved to get side-tracked from time to time. A new piece of information or request comes in or a problem rears its head and the team gets diverted from what they were doing to concentrate on this latest issue, even though it might not be the most important.

All teams involved, whether dealing with emergency response, incident management or business or IT recovery, need clear priorities and direction to enable them to operate effectively.

The business continuity plan will hopefully contain the "default" priorities, derived from the business impact analysis, although it is perfectly valid for the management team to amend them at the time, to take account of the timing of the incident or the prevailing circumstances. However, once this has been done, all those involved need to clearly understand the agreed priorities to enable them to focus their efforts on them and avoid being sidetracked.

To quote a learned business continuity practitioner, "The main thing is to keep the main thing the main thing".

Follow-up actions

This page is for you to note which tips in the previous section struck a chord and the follow-up actions you intend to take to benefit your own business continuity management programme in your own organisation.

Tip/page...	To make this tip work for me I will...

Chapter 7
Crisis Communications

Tips in this chapter:

"PPPPPPP"

"A happy media"

"Take CARE"

"Know your enemy"

"A united front"

"It ain't what you do, it's the way that you say it"

"In the news"

"Crisis communication rules, ok? (Part 1 - the dos)"

"Crisis communication rules, ok? (Part 2 - the don'ts)"

"The vacuum caused by a failure to communicate is soon filled with rumour, misrepresentation, drivel and poison."

C. Northcote Parkinson

PPPPPP...

One of the most important (and one of the most challenging) aspects of crisis or incident management is communications, both internally to your own people, and externally to your various stakeholders or the media. Get this bit right and you can save yourself an awful lot of hassle. Get it wrong and you're problems will almost certainly be made much worse.

As with Incident management and business continuity management in general, getting it right means planning in advance. Just a few of the things that can be thought through as part of this planning process include:

- Identifying your various audiences (e.g. staff, clients, business partners, suppliers, shareholders, the media and anyone else you believe to be important to your organisation);

- Ensuring alternative means of communication – don't rely on any one method, such as mobile 'phones or e-mail, but give yourself a range of options;

- Identifying the crisis media manager and support team;

- Identifying spokespeople *and training them*;

- Briefing other staff (including "front of house" staff);

- Agreeing lines of approval and clearance procedures for statements;

- Planning to ensure a consistent message, although the actual wording might differ for your various audiences;

- Keeping stakeholder contact details, press lists, etc. up to date;

- Ensuring 24-hour access to these contact details, press lists and to PR support (whether internal or external).

To use an old army adage, "Proper Planning and Preparation Prevents P... Poor Performance" (fill in the blanks yourself if you feel so inclined!). Crisis communications is an area where this is certainly true. So plan properly and make sure your communications performance is up to scratch when you need it to be.

A happy media...

These days news travels fast, and it seems that bad news travels even faster. And if the bad news is yours, depending on the type of industry you're in, the media could be upon you before you can say "news headline"!

The way you handle the media can be as important as recovering from the incident itself. There are many well-documented cases of poor media management seriously damaging a company. So it pays to be prepared. Remember, if the press want a story they'll get it, whether you contribute or not. So you need to be in a position to put your side of the story across, in the way in which you want it reported.

Make sure you nominate your official spokespeople before the event. They need to be senior figures within your organisation, but choose carefully as your managing director or chief executive may actually not be the ideal person to put in front of the cameras.

Ensure that they are given proper training in interview techniques and image management.

And finally, ensure that they have good backup, in the form of a sound crisis and media management plan, a good communications structure and the right team to support them during their time in the spotlight.

Take CARE...

When all around is chaos and the newshounds are baying at your heels, it can be very tempting to go to ground and try to avoid them, particularly if you don't feel you have much that you want to say to them. But, more often than not, that's a big mistake. If the press want a story they'll write it anyway, with or without your input.

And, in reality, you don't actually have to say that much. But the clever bit is the way that you say it. You need to get some simple, but extremely important messages across. You need to show concern, demonstrate that you're on top of the situation and put your audience's minds at rest.

A good way to remember this is to keep the mnemonic "CARE" in mind.

C is for **Concern**. Express it. Show that you're a caring organisation.

A is for **Action**. Show that you're doing something. Mention the incident management or business continuity plan. Promise an enquiry if that's appropriate.

RE is for **Reassurance**. Mention your good track record, or whatever. Let them know you're in control; that they're in safe hands.

Think "care", both when you're actually speaking to the media and when you're planning what to say, and you'll be half way there. You don't need to give much detail about the situation. But you do need to give the right message, consistently and from the top.

So, if you find yourself in the media spotlight, take CARE with what you say.

Know your enemy...

Effective media management can be crucial to effective crisis management. But the thought of having to speak to the media can strike fear into the heart of even a seasoned business manager. Journalists are often thought of as hostile or devious, but the way they treat you is largely dependent on how you treat them. Being aware of the pressures that they are under is half the battle in terms of managing them effectively.

Two things in particular to bear in mind are that the journalist is probably up against tight deadlines and is probably being paid to write a certain number of words. In other words, they have a certain amount of column inches or air time to fill and limited time in which to write their piece. They need to get a story, and they need to get it as quickly as possible. They also need to make the story interesting, so that people will want to read it. And if they can keep a story going, it can be much more profitable for them. And, believe it or not, even though you might think they're out to get you, it's not personal.

So, the more you can make the journalist's life easier, the less grief they're likely to give you. Do respond to their requests for an interview or statement – if you don't they'll just go to someone else, who may not put over the side of the story that you want reported. If you say you'll get back to them by a certain time make sure you do so. Do have *interesting* company information available in an easily digestible format (e.g. an e-mail that they can cut and paste from). Don't be aggressive or obstructive towards them, it really doesn't help. And remember, they *always* get the last word.

Knowing what makes the media tick will help you to deal with them in a way that results in the least possible hassle for everyone. And if you play your cards right, you might even get some positive publicity out of it.

A united front…

As part of their crisis management and business continuity planning efforts, many organisations quite rightly consider media communications as an essential element. As a result, they give the directors or senior managers, who may be called upon as media spokespeople, training in crisis communications and media interview techniques. This is a very good thing to do.

But how many organisations consider their "front of house" staff, such as receptionists, telephonists or security guards when drawing up their crisis communications training plans? The answer is not many. But these people may well be your "front line troops" in an emergency and may find themselves having to deal with the media because of the nature of the job they do.

A crisis communications plan is an essential part of good crisis management. And a good crisis communications plan considers all avenues. It considers not only all the likely audiences but also all those who have a role to play in putting your message across. And as part of the planning process it provides the necessary tools, including training, for all these people.

So don't neglect your front line troops. They can influence the way your organisation is perceived just as much as your top brass can.

It ain't what you do, it's the way that you say it...

The best recovery plan in the world may ultimately come to nothing if, in a real crisis, the communications aspects are handled badly.

Getting the right message across, in the right way, to your key stakeholders can be as important as the recovery activities themselves. History is littered with the casualties of poor crisis communications, with some organisations suffering severe damage to their reputation and others going out of business altogether.

So don't neglect the crisis communications plan. Ensure that team members and spokespeople are identified, properly trained and have the backup they need to keep them fully briefed when called into action.

In the news...

You've thought through your crisis communications plan, identified your various audiences, nominated, briefed and trained your media spokespeople and written some proforma holding statements.
So, if you're ever unfortunate enough to need to invoke your plan, you're all set to get your side of the story across.

But have you thought about how you'll keep an eye on what the media are actually saying about you?

As part of your crisis communications planning, you need to make provision for monitoring what's being said on the radio or TV or in the newspapers or on the internet. Therefore, your crisis communications centre should be equipped with facilities and people to enable this, including:

- TV, with recording capability, such as a video or DVD recorder;
- Radio, again with recording capability;
- A schedule of TV and radio news reports to be monitored;
- Internet access;
- A list of websites to be monitored;
- Someone to go out and buy the newspapers;
- Someone (maybe even a small team) assigned to monitor the various news reports.

And, as with many things to do with crisis management, this is best thought about and put in place *before* the event.

Crisis communication rules, ok? (Part 1 – the dos)…

When creating your crisis communications plan, when preparing to talk to the media and when actually talking to them, there are a few "golden rules" that bear careful consideration.

Do:

- Have a simple framework in place for dealing with the media in a crisis that is understood by all managers;
- Treat all media approaches seriously;
- React quickly and begin communicating at once. Take the initiative;
- Identify your various audiences and understand their communications needs;
- Communicate from as near the top of the organisation as is practicable;
- Aim to be seen as the authoritative source of information;
- Assign one person to co-ordinate media comment and another to act as spokesperson;
- Rehearse all interviews and presentations thoroughly, including (especially!) answers to awkward questions that might be asked;
- Identify "allies" who could speak positively on your behalf;
- Log everything, including times and key points of all 'phone calls or other communications. If possible, record all interviews;
- Tell the truth – you may be limited to how much you can tell, but never lie - you will be found out!
- Follow the plan, but be prepared to be flexible in responding to new information or in decision-making.

So that's the "dos", but do also consider the "don'ts" (overleaf)…

Crisis communication rules, ok? (Part 2 – the don'ts)...

The "golden rules" of crisis communications include some "dos", shown on the previous page, and some "don'ts", shown below.

Don't:

- Skimp on training. Those involved *must* have the skills necessary to carry out their roles and *must* have rehearsed them;

- Neglect any media outlet, including the regional press;

- Panic;

- Ever say "no comment". In media-land this is likely to be interpreted as "guilty as charged";

- Speculate or be drawn into apportioning blame or answering hypothetical questions;

- Fail to keep promises, or make promises you can't keep – if you say you are going to provide information, details or comment, make sure you do so;

- Say anything "off the record" – there is no such thing. Never say anything that you wouldn't want to see in print with your name against it.

Follow these rules – both the "don'ts" shown above and the "dos" on the previous page – and it's a cast-iron certainty that you'll be able to deal much more effectively with the media in a crisis.

Follow-up actions

This page is for you to note which tips in the previous section struck a chord and the follow-up actions you intend to take to benefit your own business continuity management programme in your own organisation.

Tip/page...	To make this tip work for me I will...

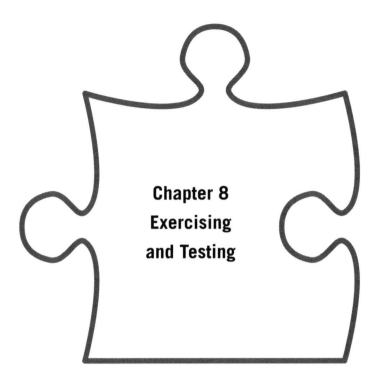

**Chapter 8
Exercising
and Testing**

Tips in this chapter:

"All the world's a stage"

"When is a test not a test?"

"Ready for action"

"Beyond the car park"

"Testing, testing"

"The whole caboodle"

"Getting the best from your test"

"Out of order?"

"Fortune favours the prepared"

"You can't prepare for everything - but you can prepare for anything."

Paul Youngjohns

All the world's a stage...

Would you expect the cast of a play to go on stage and perform without rehearsing first? Of course not! Why is it then that so many organisations write their recovery "script" then put it on the shelf without a thought for any form of rehearsal, yet expect it to work when the curtain goes up?

It is only through rehearsal that the players can learn their parts properly and that minor imperfections can be ironed out. If the script says "enter stage left" but all the action is taking place stage right, then the script should be amended *before* curtain call, not during the action.

And the more realistic you make your rehearsals, the more at ease the cast will be during the main event. So why not make a full dress rehearsal your aim.

Break a leg!

When is a test not a test?...

When it's an exercise, or a rehearsal, or a workshop. A subtle distinction maybe, but the word "test" can sometimes have undesirable connotations. It can suggest that the result will either be a pass or a fail, putting undue pressure on the participants, whereas the word "exercise" or "rehearsal" implies training and improvement.

While a problem-free test may be seen by some as "successful", this can give a false sense of security. In fact, the most successful tests or exercises are the ones that flush out all the potential problems. This allows improvements to be made to plans, processes and procedures, thereby increasing the likelihood of recovery if it ever has to be done "in anger" (or in an emergency).

So, which would you rather have?

Ready for action...

Imagine the scenario - the alarm goes off in a fire station, the fire fighters leap into action...and then start discussing what they should do next. "Who's going to the scene of the incident?", "How will we get there?", "Does anyone know how to drive that big red truck?", "Where are the hoses kept?", "Shall we use the pole or the stairs?" and "I think there's a plan somewhere - has anyone read it?"

Clearly this would be ridiculous. But, worryingly, this is not far off the mark for some organisations as regards their incident management and business continuity plans. There may be a documented plan, but no-one's actually read it, and it's never been tested. But they assume it will all work seamlessly if they ever have to activate it. In fact, what actually happens is that they completely ignore the plan and "fire fight" in the worst possible sense.

Think about it - when the fire brigade aren't putting out fires for real, they practise putting out fires, so that when they have to do it for real everyone knows what to do.

The time to find the holes in your continuity plan, or in the strategy and solutions that underpin it, isn't when you invoke it for real. So take a tip from the professionals and practise, until you're confident that everyone knows what to do and that the plan will actually work.

Beyond the car park...

One type of testing that always gets done is the fire evacuation test – because there's a legal requirement to do so. Which means that, at least once or twice a year, you have the ideal opportunity to get some added value by testing your incident management plans too, with the added benefit of a touch of realism.

In most cases, the evacuation test consists of everyone milling around the car park for five minutes then going back to work as if nothing had happened. But instead of just letting everyone troop back into the building after the evacuation test is complete, why not just whisper in the ears of one or two members of your incident management team and get them to run through the initial stages of their plans. See how successful they are at contacting the other team members amongst the chaos and confusion. Check that they actually know what to do and where to go. Check that they know where their command centre is and that they can get there (maybe even prevent them from using their cars for a bit of fun!). See if they even know where their plans are!

So, make the most of your evacuation tests. In fact, why not get the incident management team into the habit of convening every time you do one?

Testing, testing…

Some organisations think that a huge, complex, all-singing, all-dancing relocation test is the only way to prove their business continuity plan. This type of test is often costly, difficult to arrange and can be fraught with risk. For these reasons it is usually done infrequently, if at all.

But there's more than one way to test a business continuity plan. The different types of testing or exercising are many and varied and include:

- Callout tests, to ensure contact details are correct and the callout process actually works;
- "Talk through" reviews of recovery plans, to check plan contents are correct;
- Scenario-based walkthrough exercises, to familiarise team members with their roles and identify issues;
- Component tests, such as IT, communications or departmental recovery;
- Integrated tests, involving, for instance, multiple systems and/or business processes;
- Relocation tests (for both technical and business recovery);
- "Real" disaster simulations.

A sound exercising and testing strategy will involve most, if not all, of the above, conducted on a regular basis.

The whole caboodle...

Many organisations religiously test their business continuity plans, every year or every six months or even quarterly. Or at least they think they do. But many of them are deluding themselves that their testing efforts equate to proving their recovery capability.

The trouble is that for many organisations, their business continuity test is basically an IT recovery test. They recover the critical IT systems, and maybe a few other technical bits and pieces like telephony, and assume that's good enough to ensure the continuity of the business. Unfortunately, more often than not it isn't.

Of course IT is a critical component of most businesses these days. But for most businesses, there's more to running a business than just having a working IT system.

For instance, there's the *processes* that actually make the business tick - some of which are IT-related and some of which aren't. There's the dependencies within the processes, which may very well be IT-related, but there may well be other non-IT dependencies too. Then there's the small matter of people, with all their foibles, and their interaction with other people - whether it's internally within the business or externally with customers or suppliers. Oh, and there's often some paperwork involved too.

Merely testing recovery of the IT doesn't necessarily test recovery of the business processes that use it. So if you want to prove your business continuity capability, you need to think about testing the whole caboodle – end-to-end.

By all means test the component parts, including IT. But at some point you really ought to test the processes too.

Getting the best from your test...

A question that's sometimes asked by management is "why does it take several weeks to plan for a recovery test (or exercise, or rehearsal, or whatever you prefer to call it) when we wouldn't get that much notice of a real disaster?"

The answer is twofold. Firstly "risk management", i.e. ensuring that the test doesn't impact negatively on the business. While it would probably make life easier if we could just switch off the business for the duration of the test, in the real world this isn't usually possible. And we really don't want our test to be the cause of our disaster!

Secondly, we want to get the most from a finite amount of testing time and, more often than not, from the limited resources at our disposal. So we need to put a bit of effort into our planning.

To get the best from your test, you need to prepare for it properly. This means giving some serious thought, in advance, to such things as pre-test planning, risk management, test co-ordination, monitoring, reporting and follow-up activities.

Or, alternatively, you could just turn up on the day and see how successful that is.

Out of order?...

Tradition has it that incident management and/or business recovery exercising is usually done once the business continuity plan is in place. After all, how can we test the plan before it's written? Which is a fair enough question. It is, however, a bit of a narrow-minded one.

The incident management/business recovery exercise shouldn't just be seen as a means of testing the *plan*. It should also be seen as a means of developing the incident management/business recovery *capability*. In addition, it can be a great way of engaging key people and engendering support for the business continuity management programme. "Testing the plan" can almost be seen as a spin-off benefit, rather than the main event.

So why not turn tradition on its head? This may seem a bit radical to some dyed-in-the-wool BCM-ers, but why not kick off the business continuity management project with an exercise? This can be a great way of putting the business continuity plan into context, highlighting its importance, raising awareness, exercising key players and identifying issues and actions for the business continuity management programme. And if that's not enough, it also starts to develop the incident management team's capability early on in the process, which means you'll already be more prepared. So why not give it a go? You've probably got very little to lose and an awful lot to gain.

Fortune favours the prepared...

Have you ever noticed how some football teams (no names!) seem to be luckier than others?

The thing is, more often than not, it's the teams who are on top of their game that seem to get the breaks – those that are well prepared; those that think about their strategy and tactics in advance; those that train hard and practice thoroughly; those that have an effective plan and execute it efficiently. So maybe it's no coincidence that some teams seem to be luckier than others.

And there are parallels to be drawn in the business continuity world. It shouldn't come as a big surprise that organisations who are prepared; who have a plan and know how to execute it; whose key incident management and business recovery teams have had adequate training, know their roles and responsibilities, have rehearsed thoroughly and thought through the potential issues, seem to do better when crisis strikes than those who haven't.

Arnold Palmer famously said "It's a funny thing - the more I practice the luckier I get".

So, what's it going to be in your organisation? Wing it on the day or be prepared and make your own luck?

Follow-up actions

This page is for you to note which tips in the previous section struck a chord and the follow-up actions you intend to take to benefit your own business continuity management programme in your own organisation.

Tip/page...	To make this tip work for me I will...

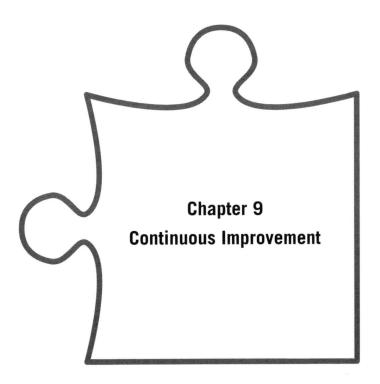

Chapter 9
Continuous Improvement

Tips in this chapter:

"When is a plan not a plan?"

"A moving target"

"A little help from your friends"

"A fresh perspective"

"A change of plan"

"Back to the future"

"Learn avidly. Question repeatedly what you have learned. Analyze it carefully. Then put what you have learned into practice intelligently."

Edward Cocker

When is a plan not a plan?...

When it hasn't been proven. Or when the assumptions it contains haven't been validated. Or when it's out of date. Or when no-one knows about it.

It sounds obvious doesn't it? But for many organisations this is the reality with their business continuity plans. All too often, plans are developed by an individual (often someone who has another "real" job too) in splendid isolation. The resulting plan gets the magical "tick in the box", but then sits on a shelf gathering dust and no-one else in the organisation really knows what it's all about. And it certainly never gets tested.

But let's not delude ourselves. An untested plan is not a plan. A plan that is based on invalid or unproven assumptions is not a plan. A plan that isn't kept up to date is not a plan. And a plan that no-one knows about is not a plan.

Your plan isn't like this is it? So prove it! If you haven't already done so, put in place a continuous improvement programme that includes regular reviews and updates, regular exercises and tests and an ongoing awareness and education campaign. In this way you'll ensure that your plan is, and remains, a proper plan.

A moving target...

You may have noticed, but the world doesn't stand still. In particular the world we do business in today is in a constant state of flux, with reorganisations, mergers, new initiatives, etc. happening all the time.

So if the world doesn't stand still, neither should your business continuity plans.

Go on, be honest, when was the last time your plans and strategies were reviewed and updated? Within the last month? The last quarter? Six months? A year? Or even longer?

If you want them to remain effective, you need to audit and "health check" your plans regularly. And you need to test and exercise them regularly too, to ensure they work as well now as when they were implemented.

The world doesn't stand still. Don't let your business continuity plans get left behind.

A little help from your friends...

Those poor old auditors often get a bad press. But honestly, your auditor is not your enemy. In fact, he or she can be one of your most important allies.

So why not make use of this valuable resource? Get them involved in reviewing your organisation's business continuity plans and strategies and validating the underlying assumptions. Ask them to observe your recovery exercises. Then enlist their help in reporting on and following up any problem areas. You will almost certainly get more co-operation from your colleagues if the auditors are involved than you will without them!

A fresh perspective...

The business impact analysis (BIA) is the cornerstone of the business continuity programme. So if you conducted one prior to developing your business continuity plans, congratulations.

However, a common mistake is to think of the BIA as a one-off exercise. It shouldn't be. It needs to be revisited from time to time to ensure plans and strategies continue to be applicable.

So you need to periodically review the BIA (or to do one if you haven't already!). It may not be necessary to perform a full-blown BIA again (unless it's been several years since the last one), but you should at least review the findings and bring it up to date.

- Think about what's changed – the way the business is organised, movements of key staff, locations, etc.;
- Check if there are any recommendations which weren't acted upon (maybe for budgetary reasons) but which still apply;
- Review recovery time and recovery point objectives;
- Confirm whether the current continuity strategies are still applicable and if not, what changes need to be made.

So, every now and again (perhaps on an annual basis), blow the dust off the BIA report and have a fresh look in light of everything that's happened since it was written.

A change of plan...

Ever heard it said that change is the only constant in business?
In many companies this is very true, but change needs to be
managed effectively if it is to benefit the organisation. And
change management is absolutely essential in business continuity
management.

Sadly it isn't uncommon that business continuity plans, produced
at great effort and expense, are allowed to become out of date
and ineffective because they are not updated when changes occur
within the business.

There are a number of changes that can invalidate your plans if
they are not trapped and acted upon. These include:

• Organisational changes (departments, business units, responsibilities);

• Personnel changes (people leaving or joining the business);

• New or changed business processes;

• Office moves;

• Changes to personal details (e.g. addresses and 'phone numbers, both
  business and private);

• Upgrades or changes to computer hardware or software;

• Upgrades or changes to plant or machinery...

...and no doubt there are others, specific to your own organisation.

So be wise *before* the event - ensure that your change management
process includes consideration of the effects on your business
continuity strategy, solutions and plans, and ensure that they are
updated promptly when significant changes occur. Your future
could depend on it.

Back to the future...

A new year (calendar or financial) is often a time for reflection, for looking back at the events of the previous year and looking forward to the year ahead with all the challenges and opportunities it might have in store.

While we shouldn't necessarily dwell too much on the past, it can be a good thing to review what's gone well and what can be improved upon, to look at what we achieved against what we'd planned to do and amend our future plans accordingly, and to look at what we can learn from our own and others' experiences.

There are lots of sources of information, both internally and externally, which can help with this process, including various reports, websites, books, magazines and maybe even some good old-fashioned networking with people who may have some valuable input or feedback.

However you decide to do it, why not resolve to set aside some time, to take stock of what's gone before and to plan ahead, before the chaos of the new year's "business as usual" activities kicks in?

Follow-up actions

This page is for you to note which tips in the previous section struck a chord and the follow-up actions you intend to take to benefit your own business continuity management programme in your own organisation.

Tip/page...	To make this tip work for me I will...

One Final Tip

Now that you've read this book you have a choice. You could put it on your bookshelf and forget about it. Or you could decide to put some of what you've read into practice.

Think about it – you now have at your disposal a portfolio of literally dozens of good ideas or pieces of sound advice, at least some of which could benefit your own business continuity management programme in your own organisation.

So why not resolve to put at least one of the tips into practice? How about that one that made you think "hmm, that's not a bad idea" when you read it? And why not do it now, while it's still fresh in your mind?

And if that works for you, why not have a go at some of the others?

What have you got to lose?

Thanks for reading and good luck with your business continuity management programme.

Acknowledgements

"Questions, questions" based on an idea by Andy Ralph of BP.

"The information gap" based on an article by Andy Mason of Sainsbury's.

"Take CARE" based on a concept developed by Magnus Carter of Mentor Consulting.

"One up, one down" and "War and peace" based on ideas by James Royds of Infosec Associates.

The author would like to thank the following people, all experienced business continuity practitioners, who kindly took the time to review and comment on the draft manuscript:

Stephen Austin MBCI, Business Continuity Consultant, Egg

Iain Ballantyne MBCI, Head of Risk Support, Masterlease

Lyndon Bird FBCI, Technical Director, Business Continuity Institute

Lesley Grimes MBCI, Business Continuity Manager, AWE

Andrew Hiles FBCI, Director, Kingswell International

Steve Mellish FBCI, Business Continuity Manager, Sainsbury's

Andy Ralph, MBCI, Business Continuity Planning Analyst, BP Integrated Supply and Trading

Robert Whitehouse MBCI, Business Continuity Consultant, Acumen

Suggested Reading

The Definitive Handbook of Business Continuity Management (second edition) – edited by Andrew Hiles (John Wiley and Sons)

Managing Communications in a Crisis – Peter Ruff and Khalid Aziz (Gower Publishing)

Business Continuity Management: A Crisis Management Approach – Dominic Elliott, Ethné Swartz and Brahim Herbane

BS25999-1 Business Continuity Management Code of Practice – British Standards Institution

Business Continuity Management: Good Practice Guidelines 2007 – The Business Continuity Institute

The Business Continuity Journal – edited by David Honour (Portal Publishing)

Useful Sources of Information

Acumen Business Services Ltd
www.acumen-bcp.co.uk
PO Box 92, Evesham, Worcs WR11 7FN
Telephone: 01386 834455

Association of British Insurers
www.abi.org.uk
51 Gresham Street, London EC2V 7HQ
Telephone: 020 7600 3333

Association of Insurance and Risk Managers
www.airmic.com
AIRMIC Secretariat, 6 Lloyd's Avenue,
London EC3N 3AX
Telephone: 020 7480 7610

British Insurance Brokers' Association (BIBA)
www.biba.org.uk
BIBA House, 14 Bevis Marks,
London EC3A 7NT

The Business Continuity Institute
www.thebci.org
10 Southview Park, Marsack Street,
Caversham RG4 5AF,
Telephone: 0870 603 8783

Business Continuity Online
www.business-continuity-online.com

CIR
www.cirmagazine.com

Continuity Central
www.continuitycentral.com

Continuity Forum
www.continuityforum.com

The Emergency Planning Society
www.emergplansoc.org.uk
The Media Centre
Culverhouse Cross, Cardiff CF5 6XJ
Telephone: 0845 600 9587

Environment Agency (UK)
www.environment-agency.gov.uk
Enquiries: 08708 506 506
Floodline: 0845 988 1188
Incident hotline: 0800 807060

Financial Services Authority
www.fsa.gov.uk
25 The North Colonnade, Canary Wharf,
London E14 5HS
Telephone: 020 7066 1000

Global Continuity
www.globalcontinuity.com

Health & Safety Executive
www.hse.gov.uk
Rose Court, 2 Southwark Bridge,
London SE1 9HS
Telephone: 020 7556 2100

Home Office
www.homeoffice.gov.uk
Direct Communications Unit
2 Marsham Street, London SW1P 4DF
Telephone: 020 7035 4848

Kable
www.kablenet.com
(*Business Continuity Magazine* and *The Source*)

London Emergency Services Liaison Panel
(LESLP) website
www.leslp.gov.uk

London Prepared
www.londonprepared.gov.uk
Melrose Avenue, Boreham Wood,
Herts WD6 2BJ
Telephone: 020 8207 2345

London Resilience Team
www.londonprepared.gov.uk
Riverwalk House, 157-161 Millbank,
London SW1P 4RR

Loss Prevention Council
www.lpc.co.uk

MI5 website
www.mi5.gov.uk

National Security Inspectorate
www.nsi.org.uk
Sentinel House, 5 Reform Road,
Maidenhead SL6 8BY
Telephone: 01628 637512

Rothstein Associates
www.rothstein.com (publishers of BC books)

UK Resilience
www.ukresilience.info
Civil Contingencies Secretariat,
10 Great George Street, London SW1P 3AE

Yahoo user groups:
UK-BCP
UK-BCP-Subscribe@egroups.com

Discussbusinesscontinuity
discussbusinesscontinuity-subscribe@ yahoogroups.com

N.B. The above information is provided for reference and
educational purposes only and should not be considered as an
endorsement of any company, product or service. All details correct
at the time of going to press.

Consultancy Services

Andy Osborne provides the following business continuity consultancy services to clients, through his company, Acumen:

- Business continuity plan health check;

- Business continuity/IT recovery capability review;

- Business impact analysis;

- Risk assessment;

- Recovery strategy/plan development;

- Emergency response/crisis management planning;

- Exercising and testing;

- Training and awareness, including courses in business continuity management and crisis communications.

To contact Andy, call 01386 834455 or e-mail him at aosborne@acumen-bcp.co.uk.

Tip of the Month

If you've found the tips in this book useful, why not subscribe to Andy Osborne's Tip of the Month and have additional tips e-mailed to you each month. To subscribe, either complete the registration form on the Acumen website (www.acumen-bcp.co.uk) or e-mail Andy at aosborne@acumen-bcp.co.uk.

What People Said...

"A great short read. Great tips for beginners and old hands like me."
Stephen Austin MBCI, Business Continuity Consultant, Egg

"It's easy to get bogged down in the detail, but this book contains easily digestible bites of good practice that too often are overlooked."
Andrew Hiles FBCI, Director, Kingswell International

"I loved this book - now why didn't I think of it? Good basic common-sense and no jargon. If you want to know what business continuity is really about I suggest you read this book ...perhaps even give a copy to your boss as a present. If he or she reads it, it might well make your life much easier."
Lyndon Bird FBCI, Technical Director, Business Continuity Institute

"Loads of good stuff in there. The style probably suits dipping in and out rather than reading from front to back, but it covers every subject."
Andy Ralph MBCI, Business Continuity Planning Analyst, BP Integrated Supply and Trading

"I found the book a good read and it was great to see that it portrayed a practical down-to-earth approach to BCM."
Bill Crichton FBCI, Business Continuity Consultancy Manager, Hewlett Packard

"The ease and simplicity of this book means that one can dip in and dip out of the different aspects of business continuity at any time. A very informative and non-technical way of getting basic answers to basic, but sometimes challenging questions. Great for those starting out or developing their understanding of business continuity management."
Steve Mellish FBCI, Business Continuity Manager, Sainsbury's

"Very readable. The sort of 'manual' that people should have on the shelf to dip in and out of – particularly when having a blank moment about how to tackle something."
Angela Robinson FBCI, Director, Garrison Continuity and Vice-Chair of the Business Continuity Institute